Education@Work

The Key to Exploit Potential

MONICA GIACCHÈ

FRANCESCO PERRONE

ISBN: 9798703574119

DEDICATION

This pamphlet is dedicated to all those professionals who are brave enough to explore the undisclosed world of real learning that develops actual value.

CONTENTS

INTRODUCTION

What you have in your hands right now is a pamphlet. Such a type of publication made its fortune in Europe between XV and XVIII centuries, when it first referred to a short piece of writing about some kind of specific topic, and then focused mainly on satirical or polemical arguments.

Even though the following communication history has turned to other types and styles of media such as papers, essays and articles that somehow overshadowed the pamphlet, it never actually died. On the contrary, its survival has gone on beneath the waves of cultural and social revolutions, and the pamphlet has landed to our contemporaneity as "a small booklet or leaflet containing information or arguments about a single subject." (Oxford Dictionary).

Far from being still something satirical or polemical, nowadays the pamphlet is a literary tool not very frequently used, but which deserves to be rediscovered. Its communicative potential is, in fact, very suitable for today's culture and society.

We live in a very fast world that changes at the speed of thought and that is full of stimuli and information like never before. People's cognitive structures are changing and are moving towards the ever stronger need to *know everything quickly*.

In the contemporary world, time contracts and differentiates by increasing the to-do list and reducing the number of hours that can be devoted to completing actions.

In order to maintain a high level of quality in the things we say, do and learn, an effort at synthesis is therefore necessary, and the pamphlet allows us to achieve it. In other words, we may say that, in today's world, the rediscovery of the pamphlet is what allows us to write and read *little but well:* it allows, not without a surplus of effort by authors, to create high quality content which can be used easily and quickly even by those who "have no time" to do so. This way, the pamphlet gives everyone the opportunity to maintain a high level of information and updates even in challenging situations.

This is, therefore, the moment to give impetus to the rediscovery and innovation of a tool that comes from the past but can be adapted to our needs, and thus maximize both its potential and the potential of its recipients.

The experiment carried out in the following pages is inspired by such a logic and embodies our idea of flexibility and innovation: if we can use our own resources in a different way, we can maximize our performance and our results.

As per the content of our work, we're about to tell you a "new story" from an unconventional point of view. We want to introduce you to an alternative approach to something that is too often considered a waste of time and money: we want to tell you what, why, where, how, and when – in our "new world" – it has turned into the true key for exploiting your potential and meet success in your personal and professional life. We want to tell you about knowledge and learning, and about their basic secrets.

In doing this, our purpose is to start a path that, we hope, may bring you towards the exploitation of your true potential, the expression of your true abilities, and the improvement of your success.

Enjoy reading!

The Key Word for Success

We spent the most of our lives supporting organizations and individuals in their development on their way towards success: from our students at university to managers from companies and public administration, from professional coachees to clients looking for help, from business organizations to political parties, we met and led hundreds of persons and groups who were constantly asking for the same category of thing: knowledge.

Whenever someone knocks on our door, they always ask the same question: *"How can I do …?"* where *"do"* stands for:

1) solve a problem,
2) achieve a goal,
3) improve happiness,
4) maximize results,
5) win a challenge,
6) obtain something,
7) become richer,
8) other things of the kind.

In other words, people consult us because they have an objective to achieve but don't "know" how to do it, i.e. they need some knowledge improvement.

And that's what we do: we provide knowledge as a main tool

for support and problem-solving; and this works!

Such a lifelong-lasting professional experience has allowed us to understand the key role played by knowledge in both personal and professional life of every human being.

Knowledge is the key word for success because it is the actual tool for autonomy and improvement.

Knowledge ultimately generates actual value that stands as a source of satisfaction for both the producer and the consumer.

> Knowledge is what enables human beings to change the *status quo* because the ability to change is based on creativity, and creativity is based on knowledge. […] Education and training are the main operational tools for knowledge improvement: they are the main tools for progress and evolution (www.alessiatiberi.com, 18th January 2021).

Only focusing on knowledge improvement can we develop that creativity that let us look at things in a different way so that we can solve old and new problems by employing our own resources originally and alternatively, and thus achieve our goals.

If we want to change effectively and maximize our performance even in crisis environments, we need to improve our knowledge!

The Unimaginable Advantage

What exactly is knowledge?

Common sense and ordinary language, i.e. day-by-day language, often use the word "knowledge" as a synonym of the word "culture" and vice versa. But actually, they are not the same thing. If we really want to use knowledge as an effective tool for success, we need to understand and appreciate the difference between these two words and between the concepts they represent.

We can say that:

> Culture is something social, i.e. it is something that is produced by groups; culture is the result of interactions and relationships between individuals who, by choice or necessity, have or put something in common, and share a certain space and a certain time. At the same time, culture is what enables groups to exist, because it represents the basic tool for interaction, communication, and relationship (Tiberi, 2020, 59-60).

At the same time, knowledge is:

> the result of actions carried out by the individual who autonomously observes, listens, thinks, experiences, remembers, re-elaborates elements of reality in order to understand the true essence of what surrounds him/her and who, possibly,

> progresses in the search for adequate solutions to real problems or for better ways to achieve goals. So, knowledge is not simply learning by heart; actually, knowledge has mainly to do with autonomous thinking, analysis of what exists, creativity, and innovation. […] knowledge is what let cultures evolve (Tiberi, 2020, 60).

In the same way, knowledge is what allows organizations, businesses and economies to evolve. It is not a trivial coincidence if nowadays we are used to refer to our contemporary society as the "knowledge society" and to our contemporary economy as the "knowledge economy", i.e. an economy where:

> […] production and services (are) based on knowledge-intensive activities that contribute to an accelerated pace of technological and scientific advance as well as equally rapid obsolescence. The key components of a knowledge economy include a greater reliance on intellectual capabilities than on physical inputs or natural resources, combined with efforts to integrate improvements in every stage of the production process, from R&D lab to the factory floor to the interface with customer. These changes are reflected in the increasing relative share of the gross domestic product that is attributable to 'intangible' capital (Powell and Snellman, 2004, 201).

And more important, knowledge and knowledge improvement resulting from a lifelong learning practice stimulate continuous innovation in every type of organization, business or firm. Knowledge and knowledge improvement, indeed, stimulate, allow, and determine

> the production of novel ideas that subsequently lead to new or improved goods and services and organizational practices (Powell and Snellman, 2004, 201).

At this point, we can easily understand that not only our economy, but our society as well are based on intellectual assets that work as both foundations and tools for success, where "success" is to be intended as:

the satisfaction of our needs and the fulfilment of our desires through the efforts we ourselves put in what we do every day (Tiberi, 2020, 1-2).

This way, if we aim at success, we must focus on the development of our skills and abilities at both an individual and collective level.

Regardless of our status of member or leader or other in whatever social or business organization, we all are involved in a continuously changing dimension that simultaneously demands and offers learning experiences and opportunities of growth.

It is up to us, either as individuals or as organizations, to proactively look for learning opportunities through education and training in different area: sometimes, even the remotest of these areas can bring us that unimaginable competitive advantage that allows us to maximize our performance!

Why?

We work thanks to our previous education, and we can "acquire" education at work.

This is, in very few words, the path that we generally follow in our life. In other words, we first attend the ordinary school (high school, university, etc.) where we learn basic elements of knowledge and develop our basic skills, and then, thanks to what we have learnt, we become a "resource" that can be employed in the economic production process. This way, our ordinary school education is "at work": it becomes productive.

In ancient times, such a level of education was enough, and life – above all professional life – followed a linear and quite rigid path: people first learnt to do things and then they used such a knowledge to perform a job that was always the same.

In ancient times, in fact, change was so slow that an entire life was not enough to experience it. And this brought people to think that things were always the same.

On the contrary, in recent times, thanks to the acceleration imprinted to life by industrial and technological revolutions, everything has become faster, even change. As a consequence, human beings now have time enough in this world to experience and consequently "know" change.

Nowadays we live in a world that literally changes at the speed of thought and implies that the ancient linear and rigid path of "school first and work then" is no longer suitable to respond to contemporary needs.

More specifically, such a linear and rigid path is no longer suitable to contemporaneity because it is no longer "enough".

"School first" remains mandatory, especially as per the acquisition of basic competences, but the pace of innovation and change is so high that a continuous learning is required for both job and life. This is that lifelong learning attitude that all of us must develop.

Before going on, let's open a parenthesis and reflect together: is the necessity of continuous learning good or bad news? Well, regardless of our status of private individuals, employees, professionals, or organizations, at a first sight, we might consider that continuous education is a "serious cost" to confront in terms of both time and money. But if we take into account the enormous benefit it brings to us in terms of improvement, autonomy, competitive advantage, etc. we can immediately appreciate it as a "good investment" because the result is worth the efforts!

This parenthesis closed, it is now time to move on in our considerations about the necessity of continuous education in both job and life. And here the main question is: "how to do it?" that stands for: "what are the channels through which we can obtain an improvement of our knowledge and skills?".

The appropriate answer depends on the specific situation. Nevertheless, we may say that there are two main types of channels:

1) the ones we turn to, personally and individually, for our own knowledge improvement. That is the case when we say to ourselves: "I think that a course or training about leadership and public speaking could help me to improve my people management skills and my influencing skills",

2) the ones we turn to as an organization that wants its members to improve their knowledge in order to maximize performance and ultimately boost results.

The second type of these channels is what we mainly refer to as "Education@Work" and it deserves a more detailed and in-depth analysis.

Where?

To correctly approach Education@Work as defined above, it is important to deal with the main aspects of its context, i.e. organizations.

Organizations are

> those groups that form themselves and keep their members together exclusively with a clearly defined goal in mind (Bauman, 1990). From this definition, it emerges that achieving the objective is the reason why the organization exists. To achieve such an objective, the organization mainly relies on the performance of its human members (translation from Tiberi, 2015, 5).

There are different types of objectives organizations can aim at. According to those types, organizations can be roughly divided into two main groups that are usually referred to as profit enterprises and non-profit enterprises:

- profit enterprises are those organizations that pursue monetary profit through the sale of goods and/or services they produce. Their income is partly used to pay production costs (employees' salary, raw materials, advertising, utilities, machinery, R&D, etc.) and partly

used to remunerate the entrepreneur's risk. In other words, they self-finance;
- non-profit enterprises are those organizations that pursue the satisfaction of needs of a community through the distribution of goods and services they produce. Their production costs are generally paid by the State.

As per the kinds of goods and/or services they produce, there is no difference between profit-enterprises and non-profit enterprises; the difference between them resides in their objectives only. A couple of examples help us to highlight such a difference: a private school is a profit enterprise, while a public school is a non-profit enterprise; in the same way, a private nursing home is a profit enterprise, while a public hospital is a non-profit enterprise. As per all of these examples, the pairs of organizations do the same things (both private and public schools are organizations where people are taught) but pursue different objectives (private schools or nursing homes aim to earn money, while public schools or hospitals aim at providing free services).

Regardless of the objectives, all the organizations have two main features in common:

1) they all produce something for someone else;
2) (above all) they all need people to realize such a production.

Therefore, production and people represent organizations' distinctive feature whatever, wherever and whenever the organization is. But while people can work at every kind of organization, production can't work without people and their brain. That's why people are the most important asset in every type of organization and, consequently, that's why the improvement of people's knowledge and skills is the basic key to the entire organization's success.

In such a context, Education@Work plays the main role in the global scenario of the investments!

What?

The concept of Education@Work refers to many different learning activities and experiences that can be theoretically grouped into different sets according to different principles.

If we analyze Education@Work on the basis of the awareness its actors have of it, we can roughly divide it into two main groups: the first is Explicit and Direct Education, while the second is Implicit and Indirect Education.

1) Explicit and Direct Education is the set of those educational paths that are structured, defined, and administrated such as formal course and classes, or on-the-job trainings. In such paths, all the actors involved (pupils, teachers or tutors, project managers, etc.) have full awareness of what they do (training sessions) and why they do it (objectives). For example, if an organization needs to improve its employees' ability to communicate effectively with external audiences, it will probably hire as an instructor someone who can plan and teach Corporate Communication and Public Speaking classes.

2) Implicit and Indirect Education is the set of those no-preplanned learning experiences that people can live in their day-by-day professional path, and that people are often unaware of. For example, if we spend our daily

routine working together with a very skilled colleague or boss, we usually acquire at least a part of his/her skills without even realizing that we are learning something.

If we look at Education@Work from the point of view of what motivates the different actors involved, we might say that:

> The motivations of the company that activates or commissions a training course are set in a clear economic dimension, aimed at achieving higher levels of quality, efficiency and productivity. The motivations of the trainees do not necessarily identify with those of the company, since the individual may be subjectively driven by other motivations such as curiosity, specific interest in the subject, the desire to grow professionally and culturally, self-love, the desire to live an emotional experience, etc. From a business point of view, this is slightly important as long as the individual's motivation, perception, and experience do not conflict with the general and specific aims of the organization itself (translation from Perrone, 2016, 8, n3).

If we consider Education@Work from the point of view of its different objectives, we can distinguish Apprenticeship Training from Education for Profession, that can be defined as follows:

1) Apprenticeship Training is the set of learning experiences aimed at letting someone learn how to perform a specific job in a specific way for a specific role. This category of learning experiences is generally intended for operational roles and is suitable to teach employees or coworkers how things are organized and arranged *inside* a specific enterprise, how the specific management wants people to perform their tasks, what are the objective the organization wants to achieve, and how it wants to meet them. Moreover, Apprenticeship Training:

> [...] is characterized by its executive objective
> which can be achieved in quite a short time:
> updates about regulatory compliance, new

action protocols, new technology, new administrative and commercial procedures, etc. [...] In other words, (Apprenticeship Training) must give clear and effective new answers to operational questions only (translation from Perrone, 2016, 11).

3) Education for Profession (sometimes referred to as Vocational Training) is the set of learning experiences that provide people with knowledge about disciplines that are relevant, more or less directly, to the development of awareness of the greater field in which a profession or a job are performed. Such learning paths sometimes appear as not strictly linked to the specific operational aspect of work but, in reality, they offer people the opportunity of coming into contact with those theoretical and practical elements of knowledge that stay at the basis of a profession, and that represent the general framework in which specific personal thinking and acting skills can be developed and improved. Education for Profession is based on the famous indispensable principle according to which:

> There is nothing more practical than a good theory (Kurt Lewin).

This way, Education for Profession is intended to provide people with the general context of inputs and tools that allow them to generate new ideas and solve new problems. In other words, Education for Profession

> offers or should offer the workers who take part in it not only information and notions but also opportunities to reflect on professional roles and functions, thus developing a line of human professional growth that goes far and beyond the strict relevance of the specific company's task. [...] (Education for

Profession) also aims at asking new questions, at arousing renewed motivation, and at opening up new horizons in favor of those who attend it (translation from Perrone, 2016, 11-12).

Becoming Part of Something Special

It is now clear that Education@Work represents the basic tool to effectively perform every kind of job and profession in every kind of role and for every kind of organization.
It is also clear that:

> In order to bring about the development of new knowledge and skills, organisations mount programmes aimed at the required information and techniques. The means whereby this is achieved is usually called training, especially if the learning programme is formally instituted by the employing organisation. Training at work can usually be divided into two types: on-the-job training and classroom-based training. On-the-job training can take the form of apprenticeship schemes on the one hand, and informal tuition from an experienced colleague on the other. Classroom-based instruction involves not so much showing the trainee how to perform a particular skill as explaining why things work, and giving instruction in how things ought to be done (Chmiel, 2001, 43-44).

Is that it? Is it nothing more than that? Absolutely, not! Education@Work is indeed something more: it is the leading way to socialize people to the organization.

Socialization is the process by which a living being learns how a group (or a society) works, so that he/she can behave accordingly and become a part of the group itself. In other words, socialization is the process by which a living being acquires the specific culture of a specific group.

We have already mentioned the concept of culture and the difference between culture and knowledge in the paragraph about *The Unimaginable Advantage*. The concepts of culture and knowledge are an essential key even here where we want to highlight that every single organization has its specific culture that models its members' behavior and that must be learnt and followed by every individual who is part of the organization itself. More specifically, the culture of an organization is:

> The set of moral, social, cultural and behavioral norms of an organization; it is based on the beliefs, attitudes and priorities of its members. [...] It is not only "understanding" but it is also "being": it is born from the often-unconscious interpretation of deep values, that are translated into principles and conceptualizations that require coherent behavior (translation from Morelli, 2003, 34-35).

Putting all those elements together, it becomes immediately clear that Education@Work, as per its inner essence and different structures, is the ideal vehicle to share organizational culture and to model its members' behavior during all their time at the organization itself.

Education@Work, in fact, gives people the opportunity of receiving information and practicing behavior about what, how, when, why, and for whom the organization works.

We must also consider that every type of Education@Work contributes to provide people with competences in four macro-areas that here we want to name: "Know", "Know-How", "Can-Be", and "Be-Aware". We can briefly describe them as follows:

1) "Know" refers to basic competencies, i.e. the set of knowledge, information, notions that are generally acquired at school and university, and that must be constantly updated through readings, courses,

  conferences, etc.

2) "Know-How" refers to technical and professional skills, i.e. the ability to use and put into practice what we have previously learnt so that we can complete a task or do a job.

3) "Can-Be" refers to transversal skills, i.e. the set of behaviors, attitudes, personal style, socio-cultural characteristics. All of this allows us to make decisions, take responsibility, choose the appropriate attitude for different personal and professional situations we come across. It also affects how we relate to the others, our tenacity and will, our courage and self-confidence, our autonomy and our creativity (Giacchè, 2016).

4) "Be-Aware" refers to our self-awareness and to the level of awareness of our role we gain through the development of our own values, opinions and beliefs.

We can therefore conclude that Education@Work is a tool for professional and organizational socialization, i.e. it is:

The variegated set of activities through which, in explicit or indirect forms and ways, the worker acquires notions and knowledge, matures values and motivations, refines skills and competences in order to acquire and consolidate his or her role in the organization. It is no coincidence that, with specific reference to the broader concept of "socialization", Gareth R. Jones, in 2007, characterized training in an openly socio-psycho-anthropological sense as *the process by which members of the organization learn the rules and internalise these unwritten rules of behaviour*. Among the many tasks that concern learning in an organization, actual training is assigned only a portion of the set of processes that lead and induce the worker to perceive himself as a member of the company. But this is an important portion which, from purely technical and operational training experiences to commercial, behavioral or managerial training programmes, plays a decisive role in shaping collective and individual identity. In any case, the common denominator of any company training experience, whether it be in the classroom, on the computer, or on the field, or on the job, consists in possessing the nature of formal, explicit and conscious socialization (translation from Perrone, 2016, 9-10).

Do It and Change, Do It and Win

Whatever one may think and talk about Education@Work, there is something no one can doubt: Education@Work is the most powerful tool to trigger change because it acts directly on the most important asset in an organization, i.e. its people.

This is not e secondary aspect because on the one hand change pushes and boosts the development of new goods and services, and on the other it represents the distinctive feature of our contemporary world. If we don't learn to change, we won't win the numerous and huge challenges our world and our markets are starting to go through.

Education@Work can support individuals and organizations in facing and positively reacting to these challenges, above all when they appear and burst heavily on the scene of personal and professional everyday life. We can't indeed forget that:

We live in the Age of Change, where innovation is a *must*. That is how it is, and how it will be, every step we'll take. [...] When things change, we tend to be afraid. We are afraid because we still don't know a lot about the *new*. When we don't know something, we can't control it, so we fear it. [...] (But) what happens if the individual (acquires) some different knowledge? Predictably enough, the individual would think, and thus behave, differently; he/she would have the possibility of thinking autonomously about the alternatives and try to react differently, to find an alternative solution, using the creativity that comes from his/her previous knowledge. [...] Knowledge is what let us [...] become active and conscious actors of our life, as well as of correct innovation, change and progress. (Tiberi, 2020, 1-61).

Managers have long experienced that if a company wants to be successful, it cannot just produce "good services and goods" that are to be sold at a competitive price through various distribution channels.

Managers now know that something more is required. But why is it required? And what is required? These are the main questions that must be answered if we want to win the challenges of our contemporaneity while looking at our immediate future as well.

Moreover, such questions must be answered in a new way. It is no secret, in fact, that things are rapidly changing in every aspect of human life, job and activity, and that previous strategies and methods of problem-solving are no longer suitable to solve new problems; such a phenomenon is so clear that it is now self-evident, and no other proofs or trials are necessary in order to grasp and accept it.

Now that we are starting to *ask the right questions*, we must try to find the right answers from a different point of view.

This way, we can say that something more is required because something more is needed, and that something more is needed because the nature of personal, social and professional life of individuals is changing at a pace never known before.

If we keep on looking at our contemporaneity like that, the question "What is required?" turns into "What is needed?". And, to answer such a question, we can start by saying that what is needed is something *different* that allows organizations to generate and develop a new and innovative competitive advantage that be able to connect to audiences as a Freedom Multiplier.
Longman Business Dictionary defines a multiplier as:

the idea that increased investment in an economy causes an even bigger increase in total income, as the spending has results that spread through the economy. Keynesians say that this is why governments should increase spending when the economy is growing too slowly, even if it produces a deficit (i.e. when the government spends more than it receives in taxes) (www.ldoceonline.com, 18th January 2021).

In the same way, we define a Freedom Multiplier as something that actually responds to the real needs of audiences, who are no longer demanding for "more" but who are constantly and increasingly demanding for "different". People no longer look for quantity, but they look for quality at a reasonable price, especially in crisis scenarios. A Freedom Multiplier is something that responds to such a need and demand, and that must be offered by organization even though it implies a different and only apparently expensive additional cost for the organization.

While the reason why such a kind of offer is only apparently expensive will be clear as long as you keep on reading, let's focus here on how we can satisfy such a demand.

How can we, individuals or organizations that we be, sell quality at reasonable prices?

In ancient times, there was two ways only: reduce the quantity and/or take advantage of employees as if they were slaves. Even though those strategies are sadly still practiced somewhere, nowadays there is no longer need for them: we have developed all we need to produce quality and distribute it to everyone at reasonable prices. Nowadays, in fact, we have the possibility of associating to our production all those immaterial links to the reality of the contexts that our audiences, consciously or unconsciously, demand. And that's the "secret" to win! That's the key aspect we must focus on to drive the change and win the challenge of our time.

Now the main question becomes: what do we mean by "associating immaterial links to the reality of the contexts that our audiences, consciously or unconsciously, demand"?

It may sound somewhat obscure but actually it isn't. It is that "something special" that we can involuntarily and spontaneously add and convey through our ordinary actions, which is immaterial, unplanned, real, valuable and reassuring, and which is capable of sharing and stimulating emotions, reasoning and actions. It is knowledge and the ability to transmit it. Thanks to them – and both are necessary – we can directly link ourselves, both as individuals and as organizations, to the contexts our audiences live in thus becoming a meaningful part of it. This way, we open a two-way street where relationships and actions start to flow in an effective and fruitful mutual way that spontaneously and by no efforts generates reciprocal advantage. There is no need for traditional advertising or influencing or persuading approach: if we behave like that towards both internal and external audiences, reciprocal advantage and win-win solutions naturally result from our daily work.

How?

If we want to implement an Education@Work path, we must understand how it works.

First, Education@Work is a process, and a process is

> a series of actions and events that develop over time to combine inputs and try to achieve goals" (Tiberi, 2020, 63).

Traditionally, such a process starts when a specific need emerges at an organization but the organization itself is not adequately equipped with tools or resources to satisfy it.

The organization turns then to suppliers that are generally represented by external specialized professionals, who analyze the needs, arrange and plan the appropriate actions, and implement them at the organization.

The organization and its suppliers are part of the same environment in which also other actors are involved (employees, managers, external customers, etc.): the larger the organization, the more complex and articulated the commitment of those who work there.

That stated, we would like to present here an innovative method of training. It is based on the consulting model by Manfred Kets de Vries and Danny Miller and it is named the *clinical* or *generative* method. The two authors argue that:

> the role of the consultant is no different from that of the
> clinician. Like the clinician, the consultant is engaged in a
> continuous dialogue with clients, in an interactive process in
> which confrontation, clarification and interpretation play a
> fundamental role [...] the acquisition of awareness takes place in
> a time-consuming process (Kets de Vries, Miller, 1992, 137).

In the following pages we will show how this fits perfectly with
the trainer and training in general.

An Innovative Approach

Kets de Vries and Miller's starting point can be summarized like that: in many strategies of managerial (but also consulting) intervention on organizations one focuses only on isolated mechanisms of the system, neglecting the complexity of human factors inherent to the operation as a whole, without reflecting, if not superficially, on the influence that all these projects will have on the culture of the organization and on the key figures that constitute it. Emphasis is placed on directly observable phenomena, but too little attention is paid to those more hidden cognitive and emotional forces that vitally influence the success of any project for change (Kets de Vries, Miller, 1992, 131).

The *generative* method, instead, considers organizational growth as a whole where change must be driven by non-directive and truly interactive methods that can involve everyone at any level of hierarchies inside and outside the organization.

If we implement such a philosophy into Education@Work, we can pave the way to different levels of learning and, as such, different levels of change in both behaviors and emotions. This way, the results will be better, in terms of both effectiveness and duration, than the ones attainable with the traditional approach because the generative method focuses on awareness, interaction, and motivation.

Generative method applied to Education@Work – which

from now onwards we will refer to as Generative Education@Work – is suitable for everyone, despite the specific role or the specific position in the organizational hierarchy. It is the more effective the more people are confronting organizational change and need to improve their managerial creativity.

Let's now go in-depth into the practical functioning of Generative Education@Work.

First, we must consider that it is a model, i.e. a sort of flexible basic method that, as such, is suitable for many and different disciplines, topics, and aspects of the organizational life and activity, from both a theoretical and operational point of view.

The more operational is the core content, the more an expert is required to support the trainer. Nevertheless, the general setting of the model requires the trainer not to give instructions like he does in a traditional class, but to help and support trainees in discussing the pre-arranged topic that can be chosen by either participants or trainers.

A group of trainees meet to discuss new ideas, analyze problems, find solutions, and then arrange an action plan for improvement.

The trainer facilitates their reciprocal communication and interaction and leads them in the generative process of creativity and problem-solving.

Such an approach requires some more time than traditional classes do, but its output has proved to be better and more valuable for both individuals directly involved and the organization they work for.

The basic scheduling requires at least three full immersion days (one per week) and, after twenty to thirty days, two follow-up sessions. Steps are set like that:

1) First day: presentation of the topic and its core aspects, negativities, strengths, opportunities, etc. The main challenge here is to maintain high focus on the topic.

2) Second day: first feedback is provided (it can be supported by tests and questionnaires) in order to highlight obtained improvement as per knowledge, awareness and engagement of the group of trainees.

3) Third day: discussion about the issues addressed. The trainer provides the group with a recap of what they did and points out an action plan for the follow-up sessions.

After twenty to thirty days, follow-up sessions take place:

4) First follow-up session: the trainer feedbacks the group through an overall summary of what they have learnt in terms of notions, their usage, effects and critical issues.

5) Second follow-up session: the trainer leads the group in a second process of discussion about the topic dealt with at the time of full immersion: such a discussion is now quicker and more effective thanks to the experience the trainees gained during the first part of the training. This is aimed at reinforcing the whole experience and consolidating trainees' improvement. A twin-questionnaire (i.e. a questionnaire that is identical to the one used at the beginning of the learning experience) can be administered in order to measure deviations and be able to assess and evaluate the increase in knowledge (Perrone, 2010).

The Generative Education@Work just described has proved to work in many different environments as both a training tool and a consulting one. It has also proved to be an extraordinary driver for change. But we can obtain such good results only if the experience is not just a one-time attempt, i.e. we can obtain good results only if the experience is inserted in a general context of lifelong learning, otherwise, it will not exploit people's potential.

Even though organizations are traditionally less flexible and change-oriented than what they say (Kets de Vrie, Miller, 1992) it is now time for them to put into practice what the majority of their managers, people and customers have already and clearly understood: if they want to change and win the challenges of our contemporary world, they must definitely open their doors to Education@Work so that they can ultimately generate actual and new value instead of simply extract it by indefinitely and anachronistically repeating and replicating old schemes:

We can't solve new problems with old tools (Tiberi, 2020, 66).

The False-Friendship of Costs

In the last three decades, social, economic and professional systems have dramatically changed under the pressure of globalization, new technologies, competition, and crisis. Education@Work has thus turned into a "must" in order to try and survive in high crowded markets with fewer and fewer customers every day.

Despite similar evidence, some organizations too often still consider Education@Work as a waste of time and money, above all if compared to ordinary production activities.

As a consequence, in many – too many – workplaces, no new skills have been developed thus considerably limiting innovation and competitiveness of those organizations that refused to invest in education and training.

But Education@Work is not a cost: it is an investment and a very profitable one!

If you think education is expensive, try ignorance[1].

---

[1] This adage is generally attributed to Derek Bok, former president of Harvard University but, according to an article published in www.quoteinvestigator.com in 2016, this is a misattribution and Bok himself disclaimed the adage. From time to time, the sentence and some of its variants have been attributed to many other different authors: Ann Landers,

Such an adage can perfectly stand alone and in forefront as a clear and effective evidence in favor of education and its consequences.

Nevertheless, we can also try an economic analysis approach as follows.

As detailed in Giacchè's essay dated 2016, traditionally, there is no structured standard of costs to refer to as per Education@Work. The only tool available is a list of cost items.

An Education@Work process consists of four steps: analysis of education/training needs, planning, delivery, evaluation.

Each of them requires an investment where is also necessary to include monetary costs for locations, materials, utilities, etc.

If we apply the traditional categorization of costs, fixed costs of a training project refer to what cannot be missing in order to deliver a course (the analysis of training needs, the teacher and the classroom) while variable costs refer to the increase or decrease of the price according to the particular and specific solution chosen among all the possibilities available as per how and where the course is arranged.

Costs that have the greatest impact on the price of the training course are related to teachers and tutors, as well as to the lack of production of the participants.

These are items that can only change based on the number of teachers or the number of participants in training courses. But we cannot think of excluding them because the essential elements of training would be missing. This way, they represent fixed costs.

We can conclude that, except for teachers, students and classrooms, all other cost items are variable.

If the training process was not commissioned by an external company but was managed entirely by the company internally by entrusting the training to a specifically hired employee or to an employee with knowledge and skills particularly suited to the

---

Char Meyers, Robert Orben, John Lubbock, P. B. de La Bruère, Rev. S. C. Morris, Charles Duncan McIver, Albert Einstein, Barack Obama. Whoever the actual author is, what we consider relevant here and elsewhere is the concept the adage vehicles.

purpose, and using the spaces normally available (for example, a meeting room used as a classroom), the process steps would remain the same, but the additional costs would be practically nil.

We can estimate the cost-per-employee and compare it with similar systems.

To do so, it is essential to know the specific costs included:

- development costs (salaries and benefits of personnel, equipment),
- direct implementation costs (training materials, technology costs, facilities, travel, equipment, salary and benefit for instructors),
- fees for participants; indirect implementation costs (general and administrative expenses),
- lost productivity and cost of filling positions during training.

When planning the annual objectives and related budgets, each company sets a series of economic targets to achieve. Part of the previous year's profit is usually reinvested. As it is generally impossible to finance every kind of investment, organizations make their decisions on the basis of the specific potential ROI (Return On Investment).

Despite the huge tradition in calculating ROI, it's not an easy job to evaluate it for Education@Work because it represents the most immaterial among all assets.

In fact, the formula is quite intuitively this:

$$ROI = \frac{economic\ benefits - course\ costs}{course\ costs} \cdot 100$$

But it's not an easy task to evaluate "economic benefits": how can we assess them?

First, we have to analyze the proper meaning of such an expression. "Economic" refers to the ability of creating actual value. Economic value is:

The energy of the economic system, i.e. its capability to do its job as both productive and consumption system (Tiberi, 2020, 22).

"Benefit" is something that actualizes "advantage". To understand this in-depth, we must go through some steps.

Goods and services have a specific relevance based especially on what they do and what they offer, i.e. a relevance based on their advantages and benefits.

Advantages are:

> [...] their theoretical abilities to solve customers' problems and meet their needs. [...] A certain advantage does not necessarily turn into a practical benefit for the customer, if the latter, for reasons beyond his control or personal choice, is not in a position to benefit from it. The fact that a sports car offers the possible advantage of fast and exciting driving does not automatically imply that a given driver will certainly benefit from it. [...] (the advantages) can be grouped into three basic types: advantages of an economic nature, which translate directly and immediately into savings or gains of money or time; advantages of a para-economic nature, which translate, albeit indirectly, into money; advantages of an extra-economic nature, which pertain to the individual sphere of personal taste, physical well-being or moral gratification (translation and adaptation from Perrone, 2001, 104-105).

Benefits are:

> [...] a positive response to a need. It is equivalent to the effective use of the advantages contained in the behavior decided to satisfy a need or, in any case, contained in the solution adopted. (The benefit) coincides with the real enjoyment of the advantages contained in the solution adopted by the customer who purchased a certain good or service. In other words, the benefit is given by the tangible and quantifiable exploitation of an advantage. [...] A first step towards the correct identification and the exact quantification of the benefits can be represented by the answer to the following questions: 1) to identify benefits

of an economic nature: "how much is the gain and/or economic savings?", "How much is the time saved?" 2) to identify benefits of a para-economic nature: "how can the economic effects of the higher safety rate be measurable?" 3) to identify benefits of an extra-economic nature: "how can the gain be measured in terms of pleasure, physical well-being or moral gratification?" (translation and adaptation from Perrone, 2001, 105-106).

"Economic benefits" consist of all the answers to the last three questions.

As per Education@Work, we can properly answer such questions if our focus is no longer on education and training as single events, isolated from the general context of the organization; we must consider them as a long-term continuous and integrated strategy for business and employees.

From such a perspective, we can assess economic benefits of Education@Work in the same way economists and companies generally assess all the other intangibles, i.e. by comparing organization's economic performance in different periods, that means comparing the economic results for the period instead of the accounting results.

Another more intuitive way to assess economic benefits of Education@Work consists in looking at it as continuous source of knowledge, innovation and change that constantly improves all the advantages of products and services, and that offers customers so many different possibilities of turning them into benefits that it is practically impossible for them not to receive at least a single one of them and/or some kind of improvement induced by them.

Conclusions

Nowadays, Education@Work has evolved and improved in all its respects: from teaching methods to training planning and management, from technology allowing distance learning to the one allowing the combination of computer-based and in-class education experiences; in other words, from concepts to forms, everything has evolved in a scientific and effective way that turns Education@Work into a structured science capable of supporting and leading contemporary epochal change in all of its respects.

Nevertheless, organizations have historically turned to it as a tool for improvement without a systemic perspective that makes it an indispensable and natural part of professional life and business continuity. On the contrary, organizations have generally considered it, from time to time, a cost surplus – especially in crisis scenarios – or, at the opposite, a one-shot miracle able to transform employees' attitudes and behaviors in just a few days: none of those approaches has anything to do with the real potential of Education@Work in terms of improvement, change, innovation and value.

We can't go on like this! The World has changed, and it is still changing at the speed of thought. If organizations don't want to be excluded from markets and competitive scenarios, they must import the logic of lifelong learning into their ordinary life, habits and strategies. That's the way to push and boost that positive attitude towards progress as the only thing capable of letting organizations survive and win the challenge of our contemporaneity.

Moreover, what has gone underestimated is Education@Work's unique power: as the origin of new skills and abilities, it is the main (not to say "the only") tool to confront and contrast economic crises that more and more frequently have been following one another since the second half of XX century. An economic crisis, in fact, ultimately means or, if you prefer, "ultimately originates from" the double-face reality according to which the needs of a specific society in a specific time have been perfectly and fully satisfied, and that such a society is ready to move on and aim at the satisfaction of a new and higher level of needs.

When targets' needs change, demand changes and offer must change accordingly in order to maintain its power of satisfaction. In other words, organizations must change and innovate themselves through an in-depth understanding of external reality and a new adequate response to their audiences' needs.

But to do so, organizations must be ready to innovate. And the only way to be constantly ready to innovate is a continuous and factual investment in knowledge improvement in every possible type of discipline, in every possible respect.

Innovation and change are not an emergency or a one-shot solution: they are − and must be − a basic part of contemporary life and jobs; and so does Education@Wok.

REFERENCES

Bauman Z., 2000, *Pensare sociologicamente*, I ed., Ipermedium Libri, Napoli.

Chmiel Nik, 2001, *Jobs, Technology and People*, Routledge, London.

Giacchè M., 2016, *La formazione aziendale come innovazione: costo o investimento?*, in Pellegrini F., Tiberi A. (a cura di), 2016, *Economia e innovazione*, FrancoAngeli, Milano.

Jones Gareth R., 2007, *Organizational Theory, Design and Change*, Pearson, USA.

Kets de Vries M., F.R. Miller D., 1992, *L'organizzazione nevrotica*, Raffaello Cortina Editore.

Morelli M., 2003, *Teoria e tecniche della comunicazione d'impresa*, Edizioni ETS, Pisa.

Perrone F., 2020, *La formazione aziendale ad orientamento generativo*, in Tempo Finanziario News, www.tempofinanziario.it (31st January 2020).

Perrone F., 2016, *La formazione aziendale: storia e prospettive*, in Tempo Finanziario, n°1, gennaio-marzo 2016, Roma.

Perrone F., 2010, *Psicologia manageriale e del lavoro*, UTET Università, Novara.

Perrone F., 2001, *Il marketing relazionale in banca*, FrancoAngeli, Milano.

Powell W.W., Snellman K., 2004, *The Knowledge Economy*, in Annual Review of Sociology (Ann. Rev. Sociol. 2004.30:199-

220, in www.annualreviews.org), Stanford University, USA.

Tiberi A., 2020, *The Age of Change: If We need Something We've never Had, We Must Do Something We've Never Done*, Amazon, USA.

Tiberi A., 2015, *EPM – Employee Performance Management*, ISEDI, Torino.

Websites

www.alessiatiberi.com

www.annualreviews.org

www.ldoceonline.com

www.quoteinvestigator.com

www.tempofinanziario.it

ABOUT THE AUTHORS

Monica Giacchè is a 15-year experience experiential trainer, project leader, and social media expert. She collaborates with Sapienza University of Rome at the Chair of Business Economics where she carries out research in Education and Training Economics. She is a member of the Board of Scientists at **POINTGLOBAL**.

Francesco Perrone, university professor, entrepreneur and expert in communication and organizational psychology and sociology, is a 40-year experience researcher, independent publicist, corporate consultant, and trainer. As a sociologist, he carries out an intense editorial, teaching, and research activity. As a clinician, he supports people in personal change, distress, or malaise. He is a member of the Board of Scientists at **POINTGLOBAL**.